There Are Way Worse Than You

Overcome All Doubts and Know that You are the Perfect Father Your Child Needs

Lewis Dunn

TABLE OF CONTENT

CHAPTER 1

LION DAD WHO IS A WORSE FATHER THAN YOU

There is a magnificent lion that goes by the name of Pascal the lion. He lives in the middle of the verdant jungle, where the sunshine shines through the leaves of the green trees. He is the unrivaled ruler of the forest, and his golden fur sparkles as it catches the sun's rays as he travels through the expansive area.

All living things, no matter how large or tiny, pay Pascal the lion respect because they understand the power and authority he has.

Pascal the lion, who always maintains a confident stance, has an air of royal bearing that is difficult to ignore. The muscles that can be seen rippling under his tawny coat are evidence of his impressive strength and agility. His amazing body. His eyes, which are a captivating amber color, exude a knowledge that can only be earned by years of experience and age. The sound of Pascal the lion's roar can be heard across the whole forest, serving as a potent declaration of his superiority.

However, Pascal the lion has another side to him, one that is concealed beneath the beautiful front that he presents. Within the boundaries of his realm lives a pride of lion cubs that are anxiously awaiting his leadership and protection. These gorgeous children, who have manes that are soft and fluffy and personalities that are full of mischief, gaze up at their father with big eyes that are filled with love and adoration.

The interactions that Pascal the lion has with his Cubs show a distinct aspect of his personality, despite the fact that he is the king of the pride. Pascal the lion's attention seems to be focused elsewhere, as though the weight of his obligations is pressing heavily on his shoulders, despite the physical grandeur and repute that he has. Because of the transitory nature of his presence in the pride, his cubs are often left longing for his attention and direction.

In this story, we go into the experience that Pascal the lion has had as a father, investigating the obstacles that he has encountered and the lessons that he has been forced to learn. As we go further into the jungle, we have a better understanding of the influence that the father's actions have on his offspring and the unforeseen ways in which this influences the course of their life.

The royal bearing of Pascal the lion conceals the fact that he is entirely focused on himself. He often prioritizes his own requirements and whims above those of his Cubs and the pride as a whole. When it comes to hunting, Pascal the lion will always make sure that he gets the most desirable piece of meat, and he will only give the leftovers to his starving young. He takes pleasure in the adoration and attention of the other animals in the forest, basking in his own grandeur without giving any thought to the effect it would have on his offspring.

The lion Pascal is preoccupied with his own pleasure, to the neglect of his responsibilities as a father. Pascal, the lion, ignores the cubs' demands for his attention or direction in order to focus on the pursuit of his own gratifications. While his cubs pine for his company and desire for his presence, he contentedly takes lengthy naps in the shade of a tree, reveling in the peace and quiet of the jungle.

The slothfulness of Pascal the lion is made clear by the fact that he avoids playing and interacting with his cubs. He doesn't bother to teach them important skills for surviving in the wild or join in on the playful activities of his cubs; instead, he sits about doing nothing while they fend for themselves. Their laughter and demands for his participation are met with deaf ears as Pascal the lion lazes about in the grass, unconcerned about meeting any of their requirements.

It is becoming more and more obvious that Pascal the lion is avoiding the obligations that come with being a dad. Because he does not offer his cubs with any direction or safeguard them from possible threats, he exposes them to the hazards that are present in the forest. Pascal, the lion, is never there when the cubs run into difficulties or roadblocks, so they are forced to figure out how to overcome the problems and barriers of life on their own.

As the plot develops, the qualities of Pascal the lion, which expose the toll they have on his bond with his Cubs, become more apparent. The cubs' lives are shaped by the effects of their father's self-centeredness and negligence, which forces them to discover their own inner fortitude and resiliency in the face of their father's failings.

The interactions that Pascal the lion had with his Cubs were characterized by avoidance and a lack of interest. Rather of participating in amusing activities or spending quality time with his little ones, he would frequently separate himself from their naiveté and boundless energy. Pascal, the lion, would disregard the excitement of the cubs when they approached him with the hopes of participating in a game or receiving instruction. Instead, he would choose to spend his time by himself. Because of this conduct, the cubs experienced feelings of rejection and insignificance in the eyes of their father.

As the cubs explored the uncharted region of the forest, they looked to their father, Pascal the lion, for direction and safety. On the other hand, he consistently ignored their requirements in spite of this fact. The cubs would turn to Pascal the lion for comfort and advice whenever they were put in a position that was either dangerous or unknown, but he would just sit there and do nothing. He would not take any action, and he would refuse to intervene or give them the direction that was necessary for their growth and their continued existence.

The absence of interaction left the cubs with the impression that they were defenseless and abandoned.

Because of his egotistical and self-centered personality, Pascal the lion placed a higher priority on his own ease and comfort than on the health and happiness of his offspring. When there were less resources available in the forest, Pascal the lion would ensure that he had food and shelter for himself, often ignoring the fact that his cubs were starving and vulnerable. He would take all of the nicest places to rest for himself, leaving his Cubs to fend for themselves in areas with less resources and less comfort. The cubs' feelings of disillusionment and abandonment were further exacerbated by the evident disrespect that was shown for their wellbeing.

The cumulative impact of Pascal the lion's avoidance, apathy, and neglect caused the cubs to feel profoundly let down and abandoned by their own father, who was supposed to provide for them. They pined for his company, sought his advice, and yearned for his devotion, but instead they were confronted with an emptiness that grew deeper with the passage of each day. The cubs started to have doubts about their value and where they belonged within the pride. They felt a feeling of desertion and developed anger against Pascal the lion as a consequence of the lack of a loving and active father figure in their lives, which generated emotional upheaval inside them.

As the cubs grew older, they turned to one another for comfort and support, which led to the development of deep connections of siblinghood. They were able to overcome the obstacles of the jungle by working together, drawing wisdom from their individual experiences, and drawing strength from the group as a whole. While they longed for their father's attention and praise, they discovered the strength within themselves to create their own paths despite the setback caused to them by Pascal the lion. This was despite the fact that they longed for their father's attention and approval.

The narrative of how Pascal the lion interacted with his cubs provides as a powerful illustration of the significance of engagement, direction, and emotional support from one's parents in the lives of their children. The lack of these necessary components left the cubs with lingering Arthurs, which molded their perceptions of love, trust, and duty. The lion cubs' ability to find power inside themselves and in their relationship as siblings shines a light on the tenacity and drive of young people who are growing up in the jungle. Despite the abandonment of their father, the lion cubs discovered strength.

Because Pascal the lion showed both neglect and apathy for his offspring, the cubs were forced to try to find their own ways and to rely on each other for assistance. As they became older, they came to the conclusion that their father would not be able to offer them with the necessary direction and protection. As part of their efforts to stay alive and develop as individuals, they were very close to their siblings, drawing comfort and fortitude from the experiences that they had in common. They worked together to overcome the obstacles that they encountered in the jungle, providing support and encouragement to one another as they discovered how to depend on their own instincts and capabilities.

The cubs had severe repercussions as a direct result of Pascal the lion's carelessness since they were forced to navigate a variety of obstacles without the assistance of their father. Because they lacked the appropriate skills and tactics that had been handed down through generations, hunting for game became an arduous undertaking for them. They encountered dangerous people, allowed themselves to be injured, and made mistakes that their parents' wise counsel and protection might have prevented them from making. They were put to the test of their resiliency and resolve when the protective presence of Pascal the lion, who lived in the bush with them, was no longer there.

In spite of the challenges they were forced to overcome, the cubs were able to pick up valuable lessons about life from their own experiences. They perfected their hunting skills, acquired strong senses, and were adept at reading the language of the forest in order to survive. They identified which plants were dangerous and which ones could be eaten via a process of elimination and trial and error. They discovered the capabilities and limits of their own bodies as they learned to adapt to a variety of environments, including varying terrains and weather conditions. The absence of Pascal the lion's leadership pushed the cubs to develop a sense of independence and resourcefulness, gaining knowledge from the difficulties they encountered along the way.

They got vital insights into the workings of nature as they watched and interacted with other creatures in the forest, which allowed them to better understand the natural world. They watched the cooperative behavior of a herd of elephants, the instincts of a mother bear to defend her cubs, and the protective care that a pack of wolves provided for their young. The cubs were able to learn valuable lessons about life from these observations, as well as from their own experiences, which helped them to build their own knowledge of responsibility and compassion.

In spite of the bitterness and anger that the cubs felt against their father, they were resolved to one day raise their own offspring in a more responsible and caring manner. Because they had direct experience with being neglected, they had a heightened awareness of the psychological toll that neglect had on their lives. They resolved to interrupt the pattern of neglect and made a commitment to one day provide love, guidance, and protection to their own children should they be blessed with children of their own.

The absence of a caring and engaged father figure left the cubs with a hole in their lives that would never be completely filled. This was the source of the cubs' misery.

On the other hand, their resolve to become better parents fuelled their desire to learn from their mistakes and look for methods to strengthen the relationships within their family. They were aware of how important it was to be there for their future cubs, to provide them with direction, and to put their health and happiness first.

As the years went by, the young lions matured into robust adults that were capable of withstanding adversity and were armed with the information and expertise they had obtained on their travels on their own. They established their own prides with a firm dedication to providing a safe and secure environment for their young, and they named such groups "prides." Their approach to parenting was molded by the lessons they gained from seeing their own father's failings, which enabled them to provide their own children the love, guidance, and protection that they had longed for as children.

In the story of Pascal the lion and his neglected cubs, the repercussions of his actions had far-reaching effects on the world. The perseverance and resiliency shown by the cubs during their path towards independence, as well as the difficulties they faced and the valuable life lessons they discovered on their own, were clear examples of how strength and fortitude can be developed in the face of adversity. Although the pain and disappointment remained, the drive to become better parents shined through, guaranteeing that the next generation would experience a new sort of dad, one that was distinguished by love, presence, and support. This would ensure that the following generation would experience a different kind of fatherhood.

The tranquility of the forest that Pascal the lion and his pride called home was abruptly shattered when an outside danger appeared on the scene. Their area was invaded by a pride of vicious nomad lions commanded by an angry alpha male called Arthur. These lions were very merciless. Arthur and his pride had their eyes set on seizing control of the situation and removing any opposition that got in their way. This unexpected threat threw a shadow over Pascal the lion's pride, filling its members with dread and anxiety as a result.

Pascal, the lion, came to come to an understanding as he saw the impending danger posed by Arthur's pride. He thought on his own irresponsible conduct and the repercussions it had brought to his Cubs as a result of his carelessness. Because the threat was so immediate, he had no choice but to address his responsibilities as a parent and the fact that he had ignored them for far too long. As the lion Pascal realized the emotional barrier he had established between himself and his cubs, he was overcome with feelings of remorse.

Pascal the lion had the fortitude to defend his Cubs when Arthur's pride began an assault on them after gaining a new knowledge of the role he was supposed to play. Pascal, the lion, let up a powerful roar just as the other lions from the opposing pride were getting closer. He wanted his pride to adopt a unified stance against the invaders. Pascal, the lion, showed tremendous courage by taking the initiative, battling off the attackers, and protecting his pride and territory in the process. He defended them with his bare teeth and claws, showing a great commitment to keep his young safe from attack.

Pascal, the lion, was having a hard time coming to terms with the consequences of his actions from the fight that was going on around him. His mind were racing. As he struggled to defend his pride, he became aware of the magnitude of his errors and the suffering he had caused to his cubs as a result of his actions. Pascal, the lion, was overcome with guilt, and as a result, his normally aggressive temperament began to change, and he began to prioritize the safety of his family above his own survival. He determined to make up for the wasted time and the emotional hurt that he had caused by making atonement for his actions.

As the conflict carried on, it became clear to the rest of the pride that Pascal the lion had experienced a change of heart. His actions, rather than his words, revealed his newly discovered passion and commitment to his roles as a parent and a leader. His actions spoke louder than words. Pascal the lion not only protected his own pride with each forceful blow he delivered against Arthur's pride, but he also displayed his regret and commitment to be a better dad with each and every one of those blows.

The most intense part of the struggle has come to a head, and the pride led by Pascal the lion has emerged triumphant. The effort by Arthur's pride to assert their dominance over the region was ultimately unsuccessful, and they were compelled to withdraw. In the aftermath, after the rush of adrenaline had worn off, Pascal the lion approached his Cubs, who were both relieved and amazed by the change that had taken place in their father. He conveyed his love and remorse to them in the form of a tender nuzzle, and he acknowledged the suffering that he had given them as a result of his negligence. like he pledged to be there for them, to guide, defend, and adore them like any loving father should, Pascal the lion's eyes welled up with tears as he said those words.

After that, Pascal the lion had a significant transformation from that point on. He was devoted to his duty as a parent, actively interacting with his offspring and giving them with the love and direction that they had yearned for throughout their lives. He took care of their physical and emotional growth while also gently teaching them the skills they would need to survive in the forest.

The lion named Pascal took the time to play, listen, and connect with each of the cubs, which resulted in the formation of a profound connection characterized by trust and devotion.

As the lion known as Pascal made his way down the road to redemption, his pride flourished under the revitalized leadership that he provided. The cubs, who had been Arthurred by neglect in the past, matured into self-assured and resolute lions, representing the teachings they had learnt through their own hardships. They established the groundwork for their own future as caring and active parents by receiving love and support from their father, who was the basis of their family.

The external danger served as a trigger in this story of Pascal the lion having a change of heart. It compelled him to face his flaws and reconsider the things that were most important to him. Pascal the lion went from being a self-absorbed and negligent parent to one who became a protector and nurturer as a result of his discovery, the heroic steps he took, and the expression of regret he had.

His journey serves as a potent reminder of the potential for personal development and transformation that exists inside everyone of us, as well as the significant influence that a parent's love and engagement can have on the lives of their children.

Following the life-altering event he had, Pascal the lion became more involved in the daily activities of his cubs in an effort to make up for the time he had neglected them. He joined them in their everyday pursuits, such as playing and discovering new things, demonstrating a real interest in their lives. Pascal, the lion, no longer shied away from their presence but instead welcomed their company and looked forward to the time spent bonding with his cubs. He became a consistent presence in our lives, providing direction, encouragement, and mental health care as needed. Pascal the lion was determined to being an engaged and attentive father to his cubs, and he did this in a variety of ways, including teaching them how to follow their prey and just being there to listen to their worries.

Pascal, the lion, had a newfound determination, and as a result, he decided to take on the role of a teacher, instructing his offspring in essential life skills and teachings. He imparted onto them his extensive knowledge of the forest and instructed them on how to successfully hunt, recognize possible hazards, and traverse unknown territory. He instilled in them a feeling of self-reliance by teaching them in a gentle manner and guiding them in a hands-on manner, which enabled them to confront the obstacles that the wilderness presented with self-assurance. Pascal the lion also highlighted the significance of togetherness among the pride, instructing them on the significance of working together, trusting one another, and providing support to one another.

In addition to this, Pascal the lion understood the value of having emotional intelligence as well as empathy. He taught his cubs how to comprehend and control their emotions by encouraging them to express their sentiments and allowing them to do so. The lion known as Pascal served as a model of compassion and goodwill for his pride, demonstrating the efficacy of empathy in fostering healthy connections both inside the pride and outside. These priceless teachings from life were the basis around which his cubs' future growth and development was built.

The pride as a whole was profoundly changed as a result of Pascal the lion's redemptive journey. The dynamics inside the pride saw a favorable change as a direct result of his revitalized passion and engagement. Pascal the lion's leadership brought cohesion and growth to a community that had previously been dispersed and unconnected. Because of his dedication to ensuring the mental health of every member, the group saw increased levels of trust and harmony as a result. The pride evolved into a tight-knit community, one that cherished and recognized support and collaboration among its members.

The shift that Pascal the lion underwent also had an effect on the other lionesses who were part of the pride. As they saw him have a change of heart and make an attempt to rebuild the links that had been broken with his cubs, they were motivated to strengthen the connections that they had with their own progeny. They worked together to establish a warm and supportive atmosphere, which would ensure the health and prosperity of the whole pride in the years to come. The redemption of Pascal the lion served as a catalyst for good transformation, which not only altered his connection with his Cubs but also altered the dynamic of the pride as a whole.

As Pascal the lion went on his path to atonement, the cubs, who had been Arthurred in the past as a result of their father's negligence, started to undergo the healing process. The cubs gained the ability to trust and forgive because to his unwavering presence, undying love, and wise direction. They acknowledged the genuineness of Pascal the lion's expressions of regret and his attempts to make amends, and as a result, their wounds started to heal over time. They regained the happiness and sense of security that comes with having a strong parental tie as they accepted their father in his new shape.

The lion cubs and Pascal set out on a trip together to repair the damage to their bond that had been done. They participated in dialogues from the heart, which enabled open communication and the expressing of their feelings in a safe environment. They shared their worries, anxieties, and hopes with Pascal the lion, and he listened attentively while offering the comfort and reassurance they had been searching for. The cubs, in turn, shared their newly acquired information and experiences, so establishing an environment conducive to the development and education of both parties.

The relationship that the lion, Pascal, had with his Cubs during the course of their lives became greater than it had ever been. They came to recognize the bravery and humility it required for their father to change, and as a result, they gained a profound feeling of respect and appreciation for their father's newfound metamorphosis. The strong relationship between them was cemented by Pascal the lion's unwavering dedication to their happiness and his persistent participation in their daily activities. Together, they constructed a future that would be characterized by love, comprehension, and experiences that they had in common.

The redemptive story of Pascal the lion demonstrates the transforming potential of development and change via the lion's active engagement in the lives of his cubs, teaching them vital life skills and lessons, and the good influence on the pride as a whole. The resilience and healing that may take place within relationships is brought to light by the fact that the cubs were able to forgive one another and renew their connection despite the presence of genuine regret and commitment. The redemptive story of Pascal the lion serves as a strong illustration of the potential for individual development as well as the significance of love and connection within the context of a family.

The resolution of our narrative marks the climax of Pascal the lion's transformation into a changed and loving dad. Pascal began our tale as a father who was negligent and focused on himself alone. The rebirth of Pascal the lion and his unwavering devotion to the care of his cubs brought about a significant transformation in both his personality and his actions. When Pascal the lion was no longer motivated by his own egotistical needs, he transformed into a dependable and supportive member of his family. A profound and unbreakable link was formed between him and his cubs as a result of his active engagement, mentoring, and unfailing affection. The metamorphosis of Pascal the lion demonstrates the power of self-reflection, development, and the ability for change that resides inside each and every one of us as individuals.

The narrative of Pascal the lion serves to emphasize how vital it is for parents to take responsibility for their children. Deep emotional scars were first produced in Pascal the lion's Cubs as a result of his neglectful and indifferent behavior toward them. The fact that he was eventually redeemed, however, exemplifies the huge influence that a caring and concerned father can have on the lives of their children. It places a strong emphasis on the significant part that parents play in determining the psychological health, growth, and development of their children. The transformation that takes place in Pascal the lion illustrates how important it is for parents to put their children's need first, to offer direction for them, and to cultivate an atmosphere that is caring and encouraging.

The parable of Pascal the lion eventually teaches a profound lesson about the potential of transformation and redemption. This demonstrates that it is never too late to change oneself and make up for errors that one has made in the past. The reader is reminded that it is possible for them to develop and grow as individuals despite of the mistakes they have made in the past by the trip that Pascal the lion takes. This gives the reader hope. It inspires people to examine their own behavior and to adopt measures that will lead to a more positive improvement in their lives. The tale of Pascal the lion shines a light and shows that it is possible to be forgiven if one feels true regret, is dedicated to making positive changes, and makes genuine attempts to do so.

As the narrative draws to a close, it instills in its audience a feeling of optimism and the conviction that individuals are capable of growing from their past experiences. The rehabilitation of Pascal the lion provides the readers with the reassurance that it is never too late to make amends for past transgressions and develop healthier connections. It sheds light on the possibility for people to develop, progress, and bring about good change not just in their own lives but also in the lives of others around them. The reader is encouraged to examine their own acts, acknowledge their share of responsibility, and work toward their own personal and emotional development as a result of reading the narrative. It instills the conviction that people are capable of overcoming their inadequacies and creating a better future if they make genuine efforts and a commitment to change in their lives.

The reader is left with a deep awareness of the transformational power of love, devotion, and change as they reach the conclusion of the narrative of Pascal the lion. It emphasizes the relevance of parental responsibility as well as the influence that it has on the lives of children. The readers are reminded of the latent capacity for development and metamorphosis that exists inside each and every one of them by the redemptive journey of Pascal the lion. The latter part of the narrative leaves the reader with a feeling of optimism and encourages them to think about the choices they've made in their own lives, be open to new experiences, and work toward being a more improved version of themselves. In the end, the story of Pascal the lion instills in its audience a faith in the transformative potential of the human spirit as well as an invitation to embark on their own personal journeys of self-discovery and redemption.

CHAPTER 2

POLAR BEAR DAD WHO IS A WORSE FATHER THAN YOU

The spectacular Arctic area may be found at the furthest extremities of the Earth, where snow-covered landscapes extend as far as the eye can see in every direction. The Arctic is a realm of ice that is home to wonderful animals that have evolved to be able to live in such a hostile and cruel environment. Our narrative is set against a mystical landscape that features snow-capped mountains, icy tundra, and glistening waterways.

A juvenile polar bear by the name of Stanley wanders about in the middle of this icy paradise. Stanley is full of curiosity and adventure. When Stanley gently walks over the ice, he is almost unnoticeable because to his brilliant white coat, which mixes in well with the icy surroundings and makes him practically invisible. He has bright blue eyes that seem to mirror the surrounding cold, and he exudes an aura that is both intelligent and fun.

Stanley is not like other polar bears because he has a ravenous appetite for information and an unquenchable curiosity in the world outside of his cold habitat. His companions often use phrases such as courageous, caring, and imbued with an adventurous spirit to characterize him. Stanley is well-known for his innate nimbleness, his mischievous antics, and his adorable routine of rolling about in the snow.

Ever since he was a little boy, Stanley has had the fantasy of settling down with a partner and having children of his own. He can already see himself showing his future cubs how to hunt, swim, and explore the huge vistas of the Arctic. On the other hand, he is also aware that it will not be a simple job for him to locate a suitable partner and successfully raise a litter of cubs.

Stanley, using the Arctic as his playground, embarks on a trip to find a companion who will share in his aspirations and experiences and will join him on these journeys. He has no idea that the journey he is about to go on would put his bravery to the test, put his ideals to the test, and teach him important lessons about life and his family.

Join Stanley on his extraordinary trip across the Arctic as the novel progresses, and watch the hardships and victories he endures on his route to finding love, becoming a father, and eventually learning the true meaning of family in this fascinating frozen region.

Stanley embarks on a journey to settle down with a partner and have a family

Stanley, brimming with enthusiasm and resoluteness, sets off on an epic journey with the intent of meeting a partner who would share his goals of starting a warm and caring family. He is aware that the Arctic is a big region, and that it will not be simple for him to locate a good companion there. As he moves on, he can't help but think of all of the fun times he will have with his offspring and how he will pass on his knowledge of the Arctic to them.

As Stanley travels across the Arctic, he is confronted with a number of obstacles that put his resiliency and tenacity to the test. He travels over perilous freezing landscapes, engages in combat with brutal blizzards, and even comes face to face with fearsome creatures. Stanley gains valuable life lessons about the importance of tenacity, adaptation, and the inherent power that exists within him as a result of these challenges.

During his travels, Stanley encounters several intelligent Arctic creatures who are willing to share their experiences and expertise with him. He learns the value of patience from an elderly arctic fox called Rebeccabite, who also instructs him on how to endure the toughest of environments. His encounter with a jovial seal called Splash, who is full of mischief, teaches him the value of friendship and working together. Stanley's character is shaped by these experiences, and he is more prepared to take on the responsibilities that lie ahead.

Stanley falls in love with a beautiful female polar bear called Monalisa, and the two of them eventually mate.
As Stanley ventures down a glacier tunnel on a fateful day, he comes across a scene that

is just magnificent. There, among the glistening ice, he comes upon a beautiful female polar bear who goes by the name Monalisa. Stanley's heart is captivated by her lovely eyes, which make her fur seem as if it were illuminated by the moon.

Stanley musters up his bravery and approaches Monalisa with the intention of making his introduction. They talk for hours about their previous experiences and their hopes and aspirations for the future as they get more acquainted with one another. As the sun sinks below the horizon, spreading a golden light over the Arctic, Stanley gets the epiphany that he has finally met the one who would complete him.

In the same way as Monalisa, Stanley had a profound effect on her. She respects his fearless attitude and can't help but see the warmth and affection in his gaze. They come to the conclusion that combining their lives and starting a family will allow them to be successful in the harsh environment of the Arctic.

In the presence of the Northern Lights, Stanley and Monalisa engage in a fun dance that serves as a metaphor for their devotion and connection to one another. They make a pact to look out for one another, encourage one another's aspirations, and provide the utmost care and affection to any future cubs they have.

It seems as if the whole world is rejoicing in the newfound peace that has been achieved by the Arctic, as the region celebrates their unification with a stunning display of colors. Because they are aware that Stanley and Monalisa's marriage will bring an influx of fresh life and happiness to their frozen world, the animals of the Arctic retell stories of love and hope to one another.

As the moon begins to rise, throwing a silvery radiance over the terrain that is blanketed in snow, Stanley and Monalisa cuddle up close, aware that their trip has only just started. They get some rest while daydreaming about the children they are going to have and the love that will keep them together for the rest of their lives.

The long-awaited moment has finally arrived: Monalisa, Stanley's devoted partner and the mother of his children, is about to give birth. As Stanley anxiously walks anxiously outside the cave, excitedly anticipating the arrival of their pups, the Arctic air is filled with an electrifying thrill.

Inside the warm and inviting den is where Monalisa witnesses the wondrous event of giving birth. She maintains her composure and tenacity during each contraction, and she has an innate understanding of how to bring her cubs into the world. Stanley sits and waits tensely, his heart racing from the excitement, delight, and anticipation that he feels at the same time.

After what seems like an eternity, the time has come for Monalisa to give birth to her first cub. They decide to call him Rebecca. Rebecca makes her debut into the world as a helpless infant, despite the fact that she is brimming with the potential for life. It's almost as if his eyes are reflecting the shimmering ice that's all around them. His eyes are glistening with interest.

Stanley has an intense surge of affection and protectiveness for Rebecca as he tenderly cradles her in his big paws. The knowledge that this cub is an extension of both him and

Monalisa fills him with a sense of immense pride. The fact that Rebecca's fur is as silky and pure white as the snow outside is evidence of the pristine splendor of living in the Arctic.

At precisely the same moment as Stanley is beginning to be amazed by Rebecca, another contraction starts to tear through Monalisa's body. The arrival of Julio, their second cub, brings their beautiful family to its full complement. The temperament of a Julio is one of calmness and gentleness, and their snowy white fur is as delicate as a Julio.

The cave is now filled with the gentle sounds of their cubs' first cries, and Stanley and Monalisa stare at their progeny with wonder as they do so. In their quest for warmth and sustenance, the young cubs snuggle up close to their mother. While reveling in the glory of parenting, Stanley and Monalisa share a look that is brimming with pride and love for their child.

When Stanley first laid eyes on his newborn pups, he was overcome with an overwhelming mixture of happiness and duty. He comes to the understanding that he is now a father and that he has been charged with the responsibility of directing and safeguarding his little ones through the difficulties of the Arctic.

Stanley's commitment to his responsibilities as a parent becomes stronger with the passage of time. He can't help but be amazed at how quickly the cubs are maturing and changing before his own eyes. He finds great amusement in their goofy antics, their fumbling efforts to walk, and their first forays into the snow.

The cubs are being educated in a variety of vital skills by Stanley and Monalisa, who take turns. They educate them on how to forage for food, how to navigate treacherous ice, and how to swim in frigid water. Stanley teaches his cubs the value of restraint and stealth, instilling in them an awareness of the world around them and an appreciation for the need to balance their use of energy with a conscious awareness of its limits.

The love that exists between Stanley and his cubs becomes stronger with each new day that passes. He takes great pleasure in the times when they press themselves up against his fur, looking for solace and warmth. As Stanley watches Rebecca and Julio develop their one-of-a-kind identities, he can't help but feel a surge of satisfaction in his own identity. The daring personality that Rebecca has mirrors his own, while the tranquil demeanor that Julio possesses brings to mind the soothing influence that Monalisa has on him.

Despite the happiness and contentment, Stanley is struggling to come to terms with a newly discovered weakness. He is always troubled by concerns over the well-being and protection of his cubs. The Arctic is a dangerous and unforgiving region that is teeming with dangerous animals and hazardous environmental conditions. As a result, Stanley's instincts to defend his family become more heightened, and he becomes determined to do whatever it takes to keep them safe.

Nevertheless, as Stanley navigates the intricacies of parenthood, he comes face to face with periods of self-doubt. He questions if he is doing enough, whether he is giving his son the direction and safety that he needs.

In the late hours of the night, while the arctic winds howl outside the den, Stanley contemplates his voyage and takes peace in the expansiveness of the starry night sky.

During these times of reflection, Stanley is able to bolster his confidence and fortify his resolve. He has come to the conclusion that the love he has for his cubs and the unshakeable commitment he has made to them is what is of the utmost importance. Stanley is aware that being a better parent is an ongoing process of education and that making errors is an unavoidable component of the path toward that goal. He makes up his mind that he will always be there for his cubs, that he would protect them, and that he will teach them the ways of the Arctic with care and compassion.

As the days evolve into weeks, and the weeks into months, Stanley throws himself wholeheartedly into his position as a parent. He finds comfort in the realization that he is not going through this ordeal by himself. Together, they create an atmosphere that is replete with love, warmth, and a spirit of exploration. Monalisa is by his side, offering support and direction.

The attachment that Stanley has with his pups continues to become stronger as time goes on. Rebecca and Julio look up to and admire their father as a source of knowledge, fortitude, and unflinching love. They regard themselves as mirror images of him. When Stanley sees how much his pups have grown and what they have accomplished, he can't help but feel a surge of pride.

When Stanley thinks back on the amazing ride that has been parenthood, he understands that the joy and responsibility of rearing his cubs have completely changed him. Because of the unbreakable tie that exists between a father and his cubs, the previously carefree and adventurous spirit that resided inside him has transformed into a power that is both loving and protective.

In spite of the initial happiness and feeling of purpose that Stanley experiences as a parent, he quickly finds that the weight of his obligations starts to fall heavily on his shoulders. As the cubs become older, they will have more specific requirements, and Stanley will start to wonder whether he will be able to meet all of those wants.

As he observes the seeming ease with which other Arctic families handle the responsibilities of fatherhood, he begins to feel inadequate and his thoughts reflect this feeling. Stanley is concerned about whether or not he have the expertise and abilities required to successfully shepherd his pups through the challenging environment of the Arctic.

As Stanley thinks more and more about the future, his uncertainty grows. He is concerned about the difficulties that are still in store for his cubs. Will they be able to negotiate the perilous sea ice and locate enough food to sustain themselves? Will they be able to endure the severe winters with the strength they now possess? Stanley is consumed by his anxieties and unanswered questions, which leads him to doubt his own ability as a parent.

His inability to sleep and general temperament are both negatively impacted by his nervousness. Stanley's restlessness and heightened state of alertness cause him to be unable of completely appreciating the fleeting times he has with his family. He is unable to free himself from the great load he has placed upon himself, and as a result, he finds himself caught up in a vortex of anxiety and self-doubt.

Because of the growing burden of his worries, Stanley unwittingly creates space between himself and his devoted partner, Monalisa, and the cubs they have together. Because he is preoccupied with his own concerns, he emotionally withdraws from others because he believes that he has to work through his issues and find answers on his own.

Monalisa, who has detected Stanley's emotional distance, makes an effort to make contact and provide assistance. She gives him confidence in his talents as a parent while also reminding him of the love and devotion they have for one another. The internal conflict that Stanley is going through, on the other hand, stops him from completely believing her reassurances, which leads to a developing schism between the two of them.

When the cubs realize that their father isn't around, they try to get his attention and love, but Stanley is preoccupied with other things, so he can't give them his complete focus. He doesn't get to experience their childlike merriment, their genuine laughing, or the happiness that should come along with raising children.

The dysfunctional distance that Stanley maintains from his family has a negative impact on their relationship. Monalisa is feeling the pressure of their troubled relationship, and she longs for the connection that they used to have. She makes an effort to convey her worries to Stanley, but he continues to maintain his distance, which makes it difficult for them to find a road to reconciliation.

The distance that separates Stanley and his family becomes wider as the days progress into weeks. The fact that he is alone himself only serves to magnify his worries and adds fuel to the fire of his self-doubt. For the sake of his loved ones as well as his own health and happiness, Stanley comes to the realization that he has to face his phobias and tear down the barricades he has built up around himself.

Stanley goes on a lonely expedition through the vast Arctic region when he is feeling alone and uncertain about himself. As he continues his journey, he eventually finds himself on a rocky beach with a sage old walrus called Wally who lives there. Wally is well respected among the other creatures of the Arctic for his vast knowledge and expertise.

Stanley, having had his curiosity awakened, approaches Wally with a combination of apprehension and hope in his heart. Wally, who can sense Stanley's inner anguish, greets him with a kind grin and encourages him to sit next to him on the smooth rocks. Stanley accepts Wally's invitation.

When Stanley opens up to Wally about the challenges he faces as a parent, Wally shows that he understands by nodding his head. He talks about his personal experiences as a father, relating stories of the difficulties and triumphs that come along with bringing up children in an arctic environment.

Wally explains to Stanley the laborious voyage that walrus parents must take in order to prevent their young from being eaten by other animals while also guiding them through perilous seas. He discusses the sacrifices that the parents make in order to provide their young children the greatest possible chance of surviving. Wally is able to portray the tremendous amount of love and commitment that is shown by parents in the Arctic via the tales he tells.

Stanley learns to understand the necessity of love, patience, and devotion in the process of being a father as he listens to Wally's tales about his experiences as a parent. The vital advice that Wally shares emphasizes the need of being there for one's family as well as accepting the difficulties that come with the responsibility of parenting small children.

He says that no one is a perfect parent and that making errors is unavoidable in the parenting role. These blunders are the means by which essential life lessons are acquired, as well as the means by which connections are solidified. Wally stresses the need for Stanley to have patience with himself and to seek consolation in the support of his partner, Monalisa, in order to get through this difficult time.

Stanley's perspective shifts as a result of Wally's statements, which cause him to reconsider his duty as a parent. He is aware that being a father is not about achieving perfection but rather about the undying love and unflinching commitment that he offers to his family. Stanley is aware that his uncertainties and worries are quite natural; nonetheless, he does not want them to prevent him from appreciating the fleeting moments he has with Monalisa and their cubs.

Stanley expresses his gratitude to Wally for his mentoring and wishes him well before parting ways with him. As he makes his way back to his loved ones, he experiences a revitalized feeling of purpose and a strengthened resolve inside his heart. He is aware that he may still have difficulties in his role as a father in the future, but with the knowledge that he has learned from Wally, he is prepared to face those difficulties with love, patience, and dedication.

Stanley comes to terms with his actions and the consequences they have on his family.

As Stanley thinks back on the discussions he's had with Wally, he gradually comes to terms with the errors he's committed in the past and the effects those errors have had on his family. The revelation slams him in the face, and an overwhelming feeling of remorse pours over him. He is aware that his lack of deliberate connection with his family and his preoccupation have contributed to the formation of a vacuum inside the family unit.

The effect that Stanley's actions have had on Monalisa and the cubs is something that he is aware of. He recognizes the yearning and the tinge of melancholy that is there in their eyes, and he is acutely aware of the need to make apologies. The burden of his errors drives him onward, fueling a passion to mend the relationships that he has unintentionally harmed by his actions.

Stanley, armed with his newly acquired wisdom and sense of direction, embarks on a trip to reunite with his family. His return causes him to approach with a sense of both eagerness and unease since he is apprehensive of how others will react to seeing him again after his absence. But he has a burning desire inside him to set things right and recover the trust and connection he previously had. This desire drives him to make things right.

As Stanley makes his way closer to the den, he gets a sight of Monalisa and the cubs frolicking in the snow together. He is able to keep his distance from them while he observes them, but his heart is filled with both happiness and desire as he does so. At this precise moment, he had an epiphany about the breadth of his affection for his family as well as the importance of their continued presence in his life.

Stanley works up the nerve to approach Monalisa as she is tending to her pups. As he gets closer to them, he notices that the expressions in their eyes are a concoction of astonishment, optimism, and caution. He takes a few moments to compose himself before speaking from the depths of his heart. He apologizes for his absence and reaffirms his determination to be the kind of father they need and deserve.

Because the genuineness of his apology moved Monalisa, she eagerly anticipates his return. She is aware that it was essential for him to go on a path of self-discovery in order for him to develop as a parent. After seeing that their father's mood had changed, the cubs approached him in a cautious manner. Stanley gets down on one knee, his eyes welling up with emotions, and he reaches out to gently hug them. In that same instant, he makes a solemn oath to himself to become a more attentive and affectionate parent.

From that point on, Stanley throws himself wholeheartedly into his part with no sign of waning commitment. He takes an active role in the rearing of Rebecca and Julio, taking part in their goofy antics, providing them with important life lessons, and showering them with love and care.

Stanley develops the skill of being present and learning to appreciate every fleeting minute spent with his loved ones. He treasures the moments of laughing and the little successes, finding happiness in the straightforward joys of seeing his cubs grow and mature. He is aware that being a parent involves more than simply giving the material things that are necessary; it also involves offering emotional support and direction.

Over the course of time, Stanley is able to see the constructive effects of his metamorphosis. The connection that he has with Monalisa continues to deepen, and the love that they both have for their cubs serves as a source of both comfort and resilience for the pair. They come together to form a loving and patient family unit, which is characterized by a strong sense of devotion.

Stanley has realized that his role as a parent is his actual purpose and has found it amid the immensity of the Arctic. He has realized that the path to being a parent is one that is replete with highs and lows, but that a parent is ultimately defined by their resiliency, love, and desire to grow alongside their children.

As Stanley gets closer to the den, he experiences a range of emotions, including optimism and worry. He finds Monalisa and the cubs nervously observing him, not knowing what to anticipate from their encounter with him. Their eyes reveal a curious combination of hesitance, doubt, and pain that hasn't quite healed yet.

Stanley is sensitive to their first apprehension and respects their want for space and time to recover. He walks up to them in a leisurely and respectful manner, his body language indicating that he is humble and sincere. He halts his approach at a reasonable distance away, giving them the space they need to evaluate his intentions.

Stanley starts to speak from the bottom of his heart, but his voice shakes as he does so. He expresses his regret to Monalisa and the cubs, stating that he is aware of the suffering he has caused and the errors he has committed. He conveys his profound affection for them as well as his unshakeable dedication to fulfilling the roles of father and partner that they should have.

As Stanley recalls the experiences that have contributed to his personal development and evolution, as well as the transition that he has accepted, his eyes flood up with tears. He emphasizes his tremendous gratitude for their presence and the pleasure it brings him by speaking about the significant influence they have had on his life. He also talks about the delight they provide him.

Stanley is aware that words, on their own, will not be sufficient to heal the wounds and restore the confidence that he has lost. He is aware that his actions speak more loudly than his words, and he is resolved to display his love and dedication by constant care and steadfast support. Moreover, he is aware that deeds speak louder than words.

He gets completely integrated into the day-to-day activities of the family and takes an active role in the development of both Rebecca and Julio. While playing with the cubs, Stanley teaches them essential skills and guides them through the obstacles of living in the Arctic.

He makes a concerted effort to be there, and he ensures that he gives each member of the family enough, high-quality attention. Stanley provides Monalisa with a sympathetic ear and an open heart while patiently listening to her story. He makes sure that their connection becomes deeper by being a trustworthy companion and participating in both the pleasures and the responsibilities of the trip that they are on together.

Stanley maintains his calm and composure throughout the conversation, which enables Monalisa and the cubs to open up about their feelings and worries without interruption. He reassures them of his unshakeable devotion to the relationship, often reminding them of his love for them and his willingness to make up for mistakes in the past.

Stanley is able to gently begin to restore the trust and ties with Monalisa and the cubs because to the continuous behaviors and real care he has shown for them. They are eyewitnesses to his development and see the breadth of his affection as well as his earnest attempts to fulfill his role as the parent and partner they need.

As time passes, the hesitance and pain that were once there begin to vanish, and in their stead emerges a revitalized feeling of togetherness and love. The relationships within the family gradually recover their warmth and harmony, with Stanley playing an essential part in the creation of an atmosphere that is caring and loving.

As the seasons change in the Arctic, Stanley and his family serve as a living example of the transformative potential of self-improvement, forgiveness, and unreserved love. They have prevailed over the difficulties and come out on the other side more powerful and more united than they were before.

Stanley, Monalisa, Rebecca, and Julio, with the help of time, patience, and steadfast determination, are able to restore their relationships and come together as a healthy and loving family unit. The scars left by the past start to go away, and in their stead emerge a profound feeling of trust, comprehension, and love.

Stanley gives his cubs unconditional affection, sound advice, and a safe haven because to the fact that he takes his position as a father very seriously. He takes pleasure in their goofy antics, rejoices in their achievements, and treasures every time that the three of them get to spend together. Because Monalisa is appreciative of Stanley's change and his devotion, she expresses her love and support for him in kind, therefore fostering the development of a healthy environment in which their cubs may flourish.

They face the difficulties of living in the Arctic together as a family, drawing strength and inspiration from one another along the way. Stanley and Monalisa work together to ensure that their cubs are prepared for the harsh realities of their habitat. They achieve this by teaching their cubs essential skills and passing on the knowledge that they have gathered over the course of their lives.

Stanley, Monalisa, Rebecca, and Julio are beginning to have a profound respect for the splendor and mysteries of the Arctic as the seasons change. They take great pleasure in the majesty of the ice-covered landscapes, the dazzling aurora borealis in the night sky, and the wealth of species that makes its home in the Arctic.

They go over the enormous landscape of the Arctic, coming across a wide variety of living things and unearthing buried riches along the way. It is important to Stanley and Monalisa that their cubs learn to have a great respect and wonder for their environment. This teaches them how to coexist peacefully with the natural world and to value the fragile balance that exists within the ecosystem.

They experience amazing moments together, such as the journey of the huge caribou herds or the exquisite dives of the Arctic seals. Together, they witness these experiences. Each new adventure strengthens their connection to their surroundings and brings to their attention the complex web of interdependent life that exists in the Arctic.

As a result of the personal growth that he has experienced, Stanley is impelled to impart the knowledge that he has gained to the other creatures who live in the Arctic. He becomes a model for individuals who are having difficulty overcoming the difficulties of fatherhood, and he provides direction and assistance to those who are in need.

Stanley brings together animals of a wide variety of species, providing a forum in which they are free to share their thoughts, feelings, and experiences with becoming parents. He relates his own experience and discusses the significance of love, tolerance, and dedication in the process of bringing up a family. Stanley exhorts them to take on their responsibilities with complete dedication and to look to their communities for assistance.

His sympathetic and empathic approach strikes a chord with the animals, motivating them to consider their own experiences as parents and to make constructive adjustments in their lives. The effects of Stanley's actions reverberate across the Arctic, resulting in the formation of a collaborative network of animals dedicated to the care of their young and the development of close ties within their families.

Stanley has a deeper appreciation for the power of his narrative and the influence it may have on others with each new encounter. Knowing that his personal hardships and progress may serve as a beacon of hope and inspiration for individuals who are experiencing problems that are comparable to those that he has faced himself gives him a sense of satisfaction.

As the narrative draws to a climax, Stanley, Monalisa, Rebecca, and Julio serve as a living demonstration of the transformational potential of love, forgiveness, and self-improvement. They have triumphed over their challenges and now have a peaceful and affectionate family despite living in the heart of the Arctic tundra.

The last several years have been a period of self-discovery, development, and repentance for Stanley. Beginning with the goal of settling down with a partner and having children, he struggled with a number of obstacles and made a number of errors along the road. However, he was able to gain vital life lessons as a result of these encounters.

As Stanley dealt with the challenges of motherhood, he first grew uncertain and overwhelmed. He began to question his capabilities and unwittingly distanced himself from Monalisa and the cubs. On the other hand, his interactions with the sage Wally and the teachings he received from the creatures of the Arctic showed him the significance of love, patience, and dedication in the process of bringing up a family.

The realization that Stanley's actions had consequences for his family brought to a shift in his perspective. He set off on a quest to reunite with Monalisa and the cubs, during which he apologized sincerely to Monalisa and the cubs and conveyed his profound love and dedication to them. As a result of his persistent activities and care, the trust and relationships between them were restored, and he developed into a more active and loving parent.

The relevance of love and family in each of our lives is brought home to us by the tale of Stanley. It places an emphasis on the fact that the ties that bind a family are not just based on blood, but also on love, mutual understanding, and a desire to develop together. The metamorphosis of Stanley proves that it is never too late to grow from one's experiences and make apologies for past transgressions.

The path to being a parent is paved with pleasures and sorrows, obstacles and opportunities for growth. To successfully traverse the complexity and to cultivate a caring atmosphere for our loved ones, we need to have love, patience, and devotion. The tale of Stanley serves as a good reminder that the benefits of being a parent are immense, and that the journey is improved when we make an effort to be present with our families and treasure the time we have together.

In a world where time may often seem like it's passing too quickly, the narrative reminds us to do things slowly, enjoy the beauty that surrounds us, and tend to the relationships that are the most important to us. It is through these connections that we discover strength, support, and genuine pleasure, thus it serves as a timely reminder to place a high priority on the relationships we have with our loved ones.

In the end, the story of Stanley and his family demonstrates to us that even when confronted with difficulties and errors, there is always opportunity for personal development, repentance, and the rekindling of romantic feelings. It is a celebration of the transformational power of family, and it serves as a reminder of how important it is to treasure and care for people we hold dear.

THE END

Made in the USA
Coppell, TX
10 June 2023